THE CONCISE
DICTIONARY OF
SCOTTISH WORDS
AND PHRASES

Crombie Jardine
PUBLISHING LIMITED
www.crombiejardine.com

Crombie Jardine
PUBLISHING LIMITED
www.crombiejardine.com

Office 2, 3 Edgar Buildings,
George Street, Bath, BA1 2FJ
www.crombiejardine.com

First published by
Crombie Jardine Publishing Limited in 2006.
This revised edition was published by Crombie Jardine in 2011.

ISBN: 978-1-906051-55-6

Written by Betty Kirkpatrick
Printed and bound in the UK

INTRODUCTION

Few people who are either native speakers of English or who have learnt English as a foreign or second language visit Scotland with any expectations of experiencing language difficulties. For the most part, their confidence is justified, provided at least they stick to the traditional tourist places and pursuits. The most difficulty they are likely to experience is with regional variations in accent and pronunciation, and that variation is true of many countries.

Discerning tourists may have some awareness of the fact the Highlands of Scotland have a language of their own, Gaelic, that is completely different from English. However, if they think about the language of lowland Scotland at all, they probably assume that this is more or less English with, perhaps, a few dialectal differences.

In this they are quite wrong. Historically, Scots is not just a dialect of English. It is a separate language, being rather a cousin of English rather than an offshoot, both languages having their roots in Anglo-Saxon. The Scots language became different in several ways from English, having, for example, noticeable vocabulary differences. For example, it was subject to linguistic influences from other languages, such as French, which did not affect English.

Scots, however, gradually lost ground to the language of Scotland's more powerful neighbour. This gradual process of anglicization led to Scots being replaced by English as the official language of Scotland. The English language then represented, as it were, the public voice of Scotland, and, as such, also became the chief literary language of Scotland.

The Union of the Crowns in 1603, when James VI of Scotland also became James I of England, was not a happy event as far as the Scots language was concerned. The Scots royal court was moved to London and the king soon showed himself to be something of an anglophile. Within a relatively short time, all published works in prose by Scots writers were in English. This was a severe blow to the Scots language, even though some verse continued to be written in Scots.

The Union of Parliaments in 1707 was an even greater blow because it led to a great increase in the contact and communication between England and Scotland. This, in turn, led to a reduction in the status of Scots, as educated and middle-class Scots adopted English as their written and formal spoken language.

Although the general tenor of formal Scots speech and writing was English, many Scots retained something of their native speech in the form of some Scots words and phrases. Some tried to rid themselves of these Scotticisms, as they were known, in an effort to sound, as they thought, more polite and less provincial. However many of these words and phrases survived for a very long time.

Some older Scots today are likely to have quite a few of these words and phrases in their speech, although these words and phrases have become fewer in number and less common as generation has succeeded generation. Many of today's younger generations may have little, or no, knowledge of them. Their language has been internationalized under the influence of the great boom in mass communication. In addition, the great electronic revolution has made many of them more likely to communicate with the Internet than with an older Scots person.

However, the Scots language has proved a sturdy entity and, at the moment, strenuous efforts are being made to promote and revive it. Let us hope these are successful.

This book contains a selection of those Scots words and phrases that are most likely still to be in use. Older people will be pleased to recognize those words that are still second nature to them and will also find pleasure in reacquainting themselves with those words that they may have forgotten. It would be good if younger people could be encouraged to learn something of their linguistic heritage which this book provides.

The book will be useful, too, to visitors to Scotland. Browsing through it will capture something of the spirit of Scotland that they might otherwise easily miss and bring to their attention the fact that Scotland has long had an identity all of its own.

In case you are puzzled over any of the spellings of Scots words in the book, it should be remembered that Scots, unlike English and most other languages, lacks a standard spelling scheme. This inevitably gives rise to the possibility of one word having several variant forms.

Betty Kirkpatrick

A

a', aw *(pronounced aw)* all: *Politicians are a'/aw the same.* [Linguistically this change from English **all** to Scots **a'** or **aw** is known as l (el) vocalization. It is also demonstrated in the difference between the Scots **ba'** and the English **ball**]

ablow below: *the cupboard ablow the stairs.*

a'body *(body pronounced as in **somebody**)* everybody: *He kens (=knows) a'body in the village.*

aboot about: *There'll be trouble aboot this.*

abune *(pronounced **abin**)* above: *the folk living abune us in the tenement.*

academy in Scotland, some secondary schools are known as **academies**: *Edinburgh Academy.*

advocate a lawyer who is qualified to plead cases in the High Court, the equivalent of a barrister in England.

ae *(rhymes with day)* one: *They've just ae son.*

aff 1. off: *Get aff the bus!* **2.** from: *He stole the money aff his boss.*

afore 1. before: *I'll be back afore you.* **2.** in front of: *She's up afore the judge the day* (=today).

ages, be ages with to be roughly the same age as someone: *His mother is ages with mine.*

agley *(literally)* squint or askew, often used figuratively meaning wrong or awry: **gang agley** to go wrong.

ahint behind: *the car ahint us.*

ain own: *That's no' (=not) his ain bike.*

aince once: *Aince there were green fields here.*

aipple apple.

airm arm: *I broke ma (=my) airm.*

airt direction, point of the compass.

aliment similar to aliment in English, maintenance, especially that paid by a spouse to someone after a divorce.

ane one: *ane thing's for sure.* [The change of vowel from the English **one** to the Scots **ane** is demonstrated in several other words, such as **alane/alone**, **bane/bone**, **stane/stone**]

anent *(now rather literary)* concerning, about: *some comments anent the court case.*

Arbroath smokie a smokie is a fish that is cured by being smoked over a fire; an **Arbroath smokie** is a small haddock which is cleaned and salted, but not split open, before being smoked. [This method of smoking fish originated near **Arbroath**, a port in the county of Angus in the east of Scotland. **Arbroath** was the location of the signing of the **Declaration of Arbroath** in 1320 which announced Scottish independence]

ashet a large oval plate of the kind used for serving a joint of meat. [The **Auld Alliance** had a linguistic effect as well as historical and cultural ones, and there are some words of French origin in Scots, like **ashet**, which are not in English. **Ashet** shares a background with **assiette**, French for a plate]

ask for the equivalent of English **ask after**, meaning to say that you want to know how someone is: *Tell your mother I was asking for her.*

at, be at it *(informal)* to be doing something dishonest or deceitful, to be up to no good: *We thought the catering manager was at it and we found him adding water to the bottles of whisky.*

athegither altogether: *We jist want to be athegither.*

atween between: *Keep this atween oorsels* (=ourselves).

aucht eight: *aucht lassies* (=girls) *in the family.*

auld old: *getting auld and frail.* **auld claes and parritch** (see **claes**).

Auld Alliance traditional links between Scotland and France that began around the thirteenth century when both countries regarded England as a common enemy and were much strengthened by the French connections of Mary Queen of Scots. She spent much of her youth in France where she was married to the heir to the French throne.

auld enemy, Auld Enemy *(often used facetiously)* the English: *We're playing the auld enemy at rugby.* [The English and the Scots were enemies for several hundred years]

auld Nick the devil: *dressed up as auld Nick on Hallowe'en.*

Auld Reekie an affectionate nickname for Edinburgh: *I was at university in Auld Reekie.* [**Reek** means smoke and Edinburgh was thought to be a particularly smoky city when all the chimneys were belching out smoke]

ava at all: *nae luck ava* (=no luck at all).

aw same as **a'**.

awa away: *The cat ran awa.* **be away tae/be away to** to go somewhere: *I'm away tae work/I'm away to work.*

awfy, awfae 1. awful: *I've got an awfy/awfae pain.* **2.** very: *awfy/awfae hot in here.*

aye 1. *(rhymes with **eye**)* yes: *Aye, I'll be at the party.* **2.** always, constantly: *He's aye been a liar* and *She's aye miserable.*

B

ba, baw a ball: *fitba.* [*See note at* **a'**]

back, at the back of (time) just after (a certain time): *The bus comes at the back of ten.*

back, come up your back to decide to do something, to feel a desire to do something: *Jim can do well in exams if it comes up his back.*

back end the later part of the year, late autumn: *Hallowe'en takes place in the back end.*

back green an area of grass, often used for drying clothes and sometimes including flowerbeds, located behind a **tenement** and shared by the owners or tenants of the flats in the tenement: *sunbathing in the back green.*

baffies slippers: *My feet are sair* (=sore); *I'm puttin on my baffies.*

bairn child: *I was just a bairn during the war.* In West Central Scotland the term **wean** is often used instead of **bairn**.

baith both: *baith buses.*

bampot *(slang)* an idiot, a fool, a crazy character: *Bob's a real bampot; don't believe a word he says.*

bane bone, if a person is said to be a **rickle o' banes** they are extremely thin: *Jean's been ill and she's just a rickle o' banes.* See **rickle**. [See note at **ane**]

bannock a kind of round flat, unsweetened cake, made from oats or barley and formerly cooked on a **girdle**. [A **Selkirk bannock** is a kind of rich fruit loaf, originating in the Borders town of Selkirk]

bap a kind of soft bread roll: *a buttered bap for breakfast.* [Now, more commonly called just **roll**]

barley-bree *(now mostly literary)* whisky. [**Bree** is the liquid in which something has been cooked or soaked and can be the basis of a soup]

barra a wheel-barrow. The slang phrase **fancy your barra** means to have a very high opinion of yourself, to be very conceited: *Tom's sure the new office girl will go out with him, but, then, he always fancies his barra.*

barrie, barry very good, very attractive, etc, a general term of approval: *We had a barrie time at the beach party.*

bauchle, bachle *(the ch is pronounced as in loch)* a term of insult used of someone very untidy: *Who let that wee bauchle in here?* [The word originally referred to a shoe or slipper that was so worn that the person wearing it had to walk in a shuffling, shambling way in order to keep it on]

bawbee originally a halfpenny, a coin which no longer exists, now a coin of small value or a small amount of money: *You won't get a bawbee out of Jock for Jean's leaving present; he's too mean.* [Historically, a **bawbee** was a silver coin worth six Scots pennies]

beastie an insect, a creepy-crawly: *There's a beastie on my sandwich.*

behoochie, bahoochie *(informal, often facetious)* the bottom or backside: *Get off your behoochie and get some work done.* [Thought to be a combination of the words **behind** and **hough** or **hoch**, the back of the thigh]

belang belong: *The car belongs tae* (=to) *Mick.*

ben 1. a mountain, now most commonly found in place-names: *Ben Nevis.* [The word comes from Gaelic **beinn**]

ben 2. in, within or into the inner part of a house: *Come way ben* or *She's ben the hoose.*

besom, bizzom a woman or girl, usually used in a derogative way: *That wee besom's late again.* [Literally a broom or sweeping brush in both Scots and English]

bide 1. if you **bide** somewhere you live there: *He bides just along the street.* **2.** to stay, in the sense of to remain: the lines from a popular Scots song *'We're no awa tae bide awa'* (=We've not gone for good).

bidie-in a person who lives with someone in a sexual relationship, although not married to them: *Anne's parents disapprove of her being a bidie-in, but she refuses to marry John;* in English mostly called a **partner**.

bing a mound of waste from mine workings [**Bings** were a blot on the landscape, but many of them have now been landscaped]

birl to spin or whirl: *dancers birling their partners* and *I felt dizzy and the room was birling round.*

black bun a type of very rich, calorific dark fruit cake encased in pastry and traditionally eaten at New Year: *Our first foot carried a bottle of whisky and a piece of black bun.*

blaeberry the bilberry: *eating juicy blueberries on the hillside.*

blate *(now mostly literary)* shy or diffident: *He was too blate to ask the lassie (=girl) to dance with him.*

blether 1. to chat or a chat: *I can't stand blethering here; I've got a lot to do* and *Let's have a blether over coffee some time.* **2.** used in a derogatory way to mean to talk nonsense: *She's blethering; there's no truth in what she says.* **3.** someone who talks at great length but does not say anything of importance: *Don't listen to him; he's just a blether.*

blootered one of several Scots words meaning very drunk: *He got absolutely blootered on his stag night.*

boak, boke 1. to vomit: *The drunk boked all over my cab.* **2.** vomit: *There's boke all over the toilet floor;* used figuratively in the phrase **gie** (=give) **someone the boke** meaning to disgust someone or to irritate someone greatly: *She's so conceited she gives me the boke.*

bocht bought: *He's bocht a car.*

body 1. *(pronounced as in **somebody**)* a person: *There's a funny-lookin' body at the door.* **2. body** can be used to refer to yourself: *Can a body no (=not) get any peace around here?*

bogie, the game's a bogie a phrase used when something, originally a child's game, has to be abandoned because it is not possible or fair for it to continue: *Not enough people have entered for the road race; the game's a bogie.*

boggin *(informal)* extremely dirty and smelly: *The toilets in that pub are boggin'*.

bogle a frightening ghost: *The bogles will get you*.

bonny *(sometimes **bonnie**)* pretty, attractive: *a bonny girl* and *a bonny view*.

bool 1. a marble or a game played with them: *kids playing bools*. **2.** a game of bowls or one of the black balls used in this: **hiv a bool in yer mou** literally have a marble in your mouth, to speak in an affectedly upper-class accent.

boorach, bourach a mess or muddle: *This kitchen's a right boorach*.

bothy nowadays a **bothy** most usually refers to a hut used for temporary shelter or overnight accommodation by mountaineers: *The weather turned nasty and the climbers made for the nearest bothy*. [Historically a **bothy** referred to permanent living accommodation for workmen, used for example by unmarried farm labourers]

bothy ballad a type of folk song, often rather bawdy in nature, which originated among farmworkers living in a **bothy** *(see previous entry)*, especially in the Northeast: a form of self-entertainment.

brae a hill, a road with a steep gradient: *The hotel's at the top of a brae and we were tired when we got there*. It is often used in place names: *Station Brae*.

brak to break: *brak his word*.

bramble a blackberry, a blackberry bush: *The children are gathering brambles*.

braw a term of general approval, lovely, fine, splendid, excellent: *It was a braw day* and *That's a braw dress*.

breeks 1. trousers: *He was wearing a pair of old breeks for gardening.* 2. underpants, knickers: *The bairn* (=child) *has wet breeks*. [A Scots form of **breeches**]

breid *(pronounced breed)* bread: *a loaf o' breid*. [This Scots/English difference in vowels is a common one, being found in such words **deid/dead, heid/head**]

bricht bright: *a bricht licht*.

bridie a type of semi-circular pasty made by folding pastry over a filling of onions and seasoned minced meat, originally made in Forfar in Angus and so sometimes still known as **Forfar bridies**.

brig a bridge, common in place names: *Brig o' Doon*.

brither brother: *sisters and brithers*.

broo, on the broo claiming unemployment benefit: *He lost his job last year and he's still on the broo*. **Broo**, or its alternative **buroo**, can apply to the benefit office, formerly called the Labour Exchange, at which people sign on for their unemployment benefit or it can mean the unemployment benefit itself. [The word is a form of **bureau**]

brose a simple dish made with oatmeal, boiling water and salt: *All the poor family could afford was a dish of brose*.

broth a kind of thick soup as in *Scotch broth* a vegetable soup, often with a meat base.

bubble 1. to weep, the expression often does not suggest much sympathy: *Meg's boyfriend's dumped her and she's spent the whole day bubbling.* **2.** an act of weeping: *She had a good bubble over the sad film.*

bubbly-jock a male turkey: *bubbly-jocks being fattened for Christmas.*

bucket 1. a dustbin: *The bin men are just emptying the buckets.* **2.** a wastepaper basket: *I put the junk mail straight into the bucket.* [As in English, it also means a pail; **take a good bucket** means to drink a lot, usually said as an indication that someone can drink a lot and not get obviously inebriated: *Jim takes a good bucket, but I've never seen him drunk*]

bum *(informal)* **1.** someone who boasts or brags a lot: *Mary's a real bum, she's always telling us how brilliant her kids are.* **2.** to brag or boast: *Pete's bumming about how much he earns.*

bumfled up, bumphled up rumpled, creased, rolled up untidily: *I'd gone to sleep in my clothes and my dress was all bumfled up.*

bunker in a kitchen, a worktop surface, especially one next to the sink: *dishes draining on the bunker.*

burn a small river, a stream or a brook: *animals getting a drink from the burn.* Often used in place names: *the Barvick Burn.*

buroo *same as* **broo**.

but often used in West Central Scotland as the last word of a sentence sometimes to contradict or qualify the rest of the sentence, but sometimes used more or less meaninglessly: *She was just as bad as he was, but.*

but and ben a type of old-fashioned cottage with just two rooms, usually a kitchen and a living room: *They brought up seven children in a but and ben.*

butterie, buttery *see* **rowie**.

byke, bike a wasp's nest.

byre a cowshed: *She was cleaning out the byre on the farm.*

C

ca' call: *They ca' him Rab.*

ca' canny to be careful or cautious: *Ca' canny on these icy roads.*

cairry carry: *cairry the bairn* (=child).

cairt a cart: *a horse and cairt.*

caller fresh: *caller herring.*

canna, cannae cannot: *We canna tell.*

canny 1. cautious, especially when it comes to spending money: *Tom's too canny to go on an expensive holiday.* **ca' canny** *see* **ca'**. **2.** gentle: mentioned in Burns' song—*Bonnie wee thing.* **3.** skilful: *a canny worker.*

carnaptious irritable, cross: *That carnaptious old man is always complaining about the kids making a noise.*

carry-out, cairry-oot 1. liquor bought from a pub or off-licence for drinking elsewhere: *We'll get a carry-out on the way to the party.* **2.** food bought in a restaurant to be eaten elsewhere: *I'm too tired to cook, let's get a carry-out.* **3.** a restaurant which sells food that can be eaten off the premises: *There's a Chinese carry-out on the High Street.*

cast something up to someone if you **cast something up to someone** you reproach them with something or remind them of something that they have done or said that they would rather forget: *Last year she was fined for speeding and her sister keeps casting it up.*

cauld cold: *a cauld, snowy day.*

causey a cobbled street or road, sometimes used for a paved road.
causey stane a cobble stone, sometimes used for a paving stone.

ceilidh *(pronounced **kale**-ee)* a social gathering, originally informal, but now sometimes more formal, with traditional music, singing and dancing: *Bob played his fiddle at the ceilidh in the village hall.*

ceud mile failte *(pronounced **kee**-ut **mee**-luh **fah-ill**-tya)* a Gaelic phrase, rather than a Scots one, but very commonly seen on signs in Scotland to welcome visitors. It means literally a hundred thousand welcomes.

champit *(used of vegetables)* mashed: *champit tatties* (=potatoes).

chanty a chamber pot: *a chanty under the bed.*

chap 1. to knock on a door or a window. **2.** a knock: *There was a chap at the door.*

chiel *(now mostly literary)* a man, especially a young man, a fellow. [Popularized by the famous line from Burns *'a chiel amang* (=among) *us takin' notes'*]

chitter to shiver with cold: *It was freezing cold and the children were chittering.*

chittering bite a snack eaten immediately after a swim, supposedly to reduce the chances of getting a cold.

chuckie stane a small stone or pebble: *He threw a chuckie stane into the sea.*

chum to accompany a friend somewhere: *Will you chum me to the corner shop?*

clachan a small village: *It's a wee isolated clachan now uninhabited.*

claes clothes: *She was wearing her best claes*. **auld claes and parritch** a return to a normal, ordinary way of life after experiencing something unusual, celebratory or indulgent: *We're back from our cruise now and it's a case of auld claes and parritch.*

clamjamfrie, clanjamrie 1. *(mostly used in a derogatory way)* a group of people: *a clamjamfrie of noisy teenagers gathered on the beach.* **2.** an assortment of things, a mixed bag: *the clamjamfrie that you get at car boot sales.*

clap to give an animal a friendly pat: *Clap the puppy!*

clapshot potatoes and turnips (neeps) which have been cooked and mashed together.

clarty extremely dirty: *Wash those clarty hands before you eat.* [From **clart** mud or a lump of something dirty or unpleasant]

cleek a hook or a hook-shaped device: *put a cleek in the wall to hang the picture on.*

cleg a horse fly which gives a particularly vicious bite.

clishmaclaver *(now often literary)* idle or incessant talk, gossip.

cloot a piece of cloth, often a cloth used for a particular purpose: *a dish cloot*. **clootie dumpling** *see* **dumpling**.

close 1. *(often used in place names)* a passageway or lane leading off a main street: *Mary King's Close in Edinburgh*. **2.** a passageway that connects a group of houses to a main street. **3.** in the Glasgow area, the entry passage and stairway in a tenement; also the group of flats sharing this entry passage and stairway: *the tenement close he lived in as a child.*

cludgie *(informal)* a toilet: *The cludgie in that pub's filthy.*

clype, clipe 1. to tell tales: *He clyped on wee Jimmie to the teacher.* **2.** someone who tells tales: *That wee clype told my mother I wasn't at school.*

cock-a-leekie a kind of soup made with a fowl, often chicken, and leeks, sometimes with the addition of prunes or onions.

coggle to wobble, to rock, to be unsteady: *The table was cogglin'.*

coggly wobbly, unsteady: *a coggly table.*

collop a thin slice of meat fried in a pan.

conceit, have a good conceit of yourself to have a very high opinion of yourself: *No one thinks that he has a chance of winning, but he himself has a good conceit of himself.*

coo a cow: *The coos in the byre* (=cowshed) *were restless.*

cookie a kind of round slightly sweet bun made using yeast: *a cream cookie.* [The American **cookie,** a sweet biscuit, is completely different]

coorie doon to snuggle up: *The child cooried doon on the pile of blankets and fell asleep.*

coorse coarse **1.** *(of weather)* extremely unpleasant, stormy: *It was coorse weather to be sailing in.* **2.** *(of a person)* rough, awkward: *Jack's new girlfriend is a bit coorse.* **3.** *(of a person)* bad, wicked.

corbie a crow, a raven.

corrie a round-shaped hollow in the side of a mountain or between mountains.

couthie, couthy 1. unsophisticated, unpretentious, homely: *That was regarded as too couthie for the fashionable city scene.* **2.** comfortable, snug, neat: *He built a couthie wee cottage for his family.* **3.** *(of a person)* friendly, sociable, sympathetic: *They were lucky enough to have couthie neighbours.*

cowp, coup 1. to overturn, to upset; to fall over: *Watch out; you'll coup the boat.* **2.** a rubbish tip.

crabbit bad-tempered, cross; in a bad temper, grumpy: *Jack's crabbit because he has a hangover.*

crack conversation, chat, gossip, news: *Come in and gie (=give) us your crack.*

cranachan a popular Scottish dessert made from cream, honey, soft oatmeal and raspberries, sometimes with the addition of **crowdie** and/or whisky.

craw 1. a crow. **2.** to crow, to boast: *He's crawin' about his new job.*

creel a large basket: *fisherwomen selling fish from their creels.*

crivvens an exclamation of surprise: *Crivvens, where did you spring from?*

croft a smallholding, especially one in the Highlands and Islands, run by a **crofter**.

crowdie a kind of soft white cheese.

crummock a shepherd's crook with a curved head.

cry call or name: *They cried the baby Kate.*

cuddy, cuddie a donkey; a horse. **cuddyback** a ride on someone's shoulders: *The child was tired and her daddy gave her a cuddyback.*

Cullen skink a kind of fish soup made from smoked haddock, potatoes, onions and milk. [Named after the fishing village of **Cullen** on the Moray Firth; **skink** itself is a soup made from a boiled shin of beef]

cundie, condie a gutter at the side of a road; a drain; the cover of a drain: *He dropped the watch and it fell down the cundie.*

D

dab, let dab *(informal)* to let something be known, to reveal something: *She had a big win on the lottery and never let dab.*

dae do: *Can we dae it in time?* [The vowel change shown in **dae/do** is quite a common one and is shown in such words as **nae/no**, **sae/so**]

daft, be daft on, daft aboot *(informal)* extremely keen on someone or something, mad about someone or something: *The child's daft on swimming* and *Jim's daft on Mary.*

dander, dauner stroll: *I'm going for a dander before breakfast* and *We dandered along the shore.*

daud, dod a lump: *a daud o' cheese.*

daur dare: *Wha (=who) daur meddle w' (=with) me?*

day, the day today: *It's a school holiday the day.*

deave to annoy or irritate someone with too much talking or noise: *The kids were deaving us with demands for ice cream.*

deid dead: *their deid comrades.*

deil the devil: Burns' song *The deil's awa wi the Exciseman.*

deochandorous a drink taken before departure, rather along the lines of **one for the road,** but much more romantic sounding: the song *Just a wee deochandorous* popularized by the Scots comedian/singer Harry Lauder.

dicht wipe: *I'll give the kitchen table a quick dicht* and *Dicht the baby's face.*

ding doon to rain very heavily: *It dinged doon a* (=all) *day.*

dinger, go your dinger 1. to give full vent to your anger: *Mum'll go her dinger if we're late again.* **2.** to do something with great enthusiasm: *The pianist was going his dinger for most of the party.* [From the verb **ding** to strike or beat]

dinna, dinnae do not: *I dinna ken* (=I don't know).

dirk a kind of short dagger worn by Highland warriors and now part of formal Highland dress.

disjaskit miserable, downcast: *disjaskit when her lover went away.*

disna, disnae does not: *She disnae stay here.*

dochter daughter: *They've three sons and a dochter.*

docken 1. the dock plant or a leaf from it: *Docken is said to soothe nettle stings.* **2.** something of little or no value, a whit: *He doesn't care* *a docken about his work.*

dod *same as* **daud**.

doitit not of sound mind, foolish: *He must have been doitit to take such a risk.*

donnert not mentally alert, stupid: *The old man's gettin' a bit donnert.*

dook bathe: *It's hot and we're goin' for a dook in the sea.* [To **dook for apples** at Hallowe'en is to try to pick apples out of a bowl of water using your teeth or, occasionally, a fork]

doon down: *doon the road.* [In the Glasgow area, in the summer, many people used to go **doon the watter**, that is down the water of the River Clyde, in pleasure steamers to the resorts on the coast, such as Rothesay; *see* **watter**]

doot **1.** doubt: *Ahe hae ma doots* (=I have my doubts). **2.** to be inclined to believe, to fear: *Ah doot he's deid* (=I think he's dead).

douce *(mostly now applied to places)* quiet, sedate: *Riots are unknown in this douce suburb of the city.* [One of several Scots words that have French connections (*see* **ashet**). In Scots **douce** originally meant sweet or pleasant and has obvious connections with the French **douce**, feminine of **doux**]

dour *(rhymes with poor)* humourless, reserved and sullen: *a dour old woman, never known to smile.*

dowt a cigarette end: *an old tramp picking up dowts in the street.*

dram a drink, especially a drink of whisky: *There's a pub over there; let's have a dram.*

drap drop: *add a wee drap o' water* and *She drapped the milk bottle.*

dree to suffer or endure, commonly found in the expression **dree your weird** which means that you will just have to put up with whatever fate brings you.

dreich *(now most usually applied to the weather)* miserable, depressing, bleak: *a typical dreich November day*; no other word, whether in Scots or English, so aptly describes the kind of wet, dark, depressing day which makes you want to stay in bed.

drookit completely soaked, drenched, but somehow sounding much wetter than either of these: *It started to pour suddenly and we got drookit.*

drop scone a Scots pancake. *See* **pancake**.

dross very small pieces of coal; coal dust: *We need some more coal; there's only dross left.*

drouth, drooth thirst, often a thirst for liquor: *He had a drouth on him and he made for the nearest pub.* [A form of the English word **drought**]

drouthy thirsty, often thirsty for liquor; also used to refer to someone who has a particular fondness for alcohol: *drouthy old men making for the pub.*

dug dog: *stray dugs ripping the rubbish sacks.*

dumpling a kind of rich fruit pudding cooked by boiling or steaming. A **clootie dumpling** is one that is wrapped in a **cloot** (=piece of cloth) and cooked in this.

dumps, give someone their dumps to give someone, usually a child, a series of thumps on the back as a supposed celebration of their birthday, one thump being given for each year.

dunny a cellar or underground passage in a **tenement**: *storing things in the dunny*.

dunt 1. a heavy blow, a knock: *He fell downstairs and got a bad dunt on the head*. **2.** to strike, to bump, to knock: *He dunted his heid on the low ceiling beams*.

dux in some Scottish schools, the pupil who gets the best academic results in a class or in the whole school: *Jim was presented with a gold medal for being dux of the school*. [From the Latin word **dux**, a leader]

dwam, in a dwam in a daydream, distracted: *Jean's in a dwam; she hasn't heard a word I've said*.

dyke a low stone wall of the kind used to separate fields from each other or to enclose gardens: *The sheep escaped through a hole in the dyke*.

E

eariewig an earwig.

easy-osy, easy-oasy extremely easy-going, laid-back: *Anybody else would have lost their temper, but Jack's very easy-osy*.

echt eight: *at echt o'clock*.

Edinburgh rock a kind of sweet consisting of brittle, pastel-coloured, flavoured sticks: *We bought some boxes of Edinburgh rock as a souvenir of Scotland*. [So-called because first made in Edinburgh]

ee an eye: *He's got a black ee*.

eejit idiot: *Bob was a right eejit to believe her story.*

een eyes, plural of **ee**: *a pair o' sparkling een.*

efter after: *look efter the bairns* (=children) *and one efter the ither* (=other).

efternuin, efternin afternoon: *two in the efternuin.*

eldritch *(now mostly literary)* weird, unearthly, ghostly: *Suddenly we heard an eldritch scream.*

export a kind of strong beer which is slightly darker in colour then **heavy**.

F

fae, frae from: *She's fae Ayr.*

fair very: *I wis fair exhausted.*

faither father: *faither and son.* [The phrase **I kent his faither**, literally means I knew his father, but it is commonly used as a kind of put-down to cut someone down to size, the implication being that, if you knew his father, he cannot be all that important]

fankle a tangle, muddle. **Get in a fankle** to get into a state of confusion: *I tried to install my new computer myself and got into a real fankle.*

fantoosh ostentatious, pretentious, flashy: *She came to the children's picnic wearing a ridiculously fantoosh dress.*

fash, dinna fash yersel means either do not get annoyed: *Dinna fash yersel; the child hit you by accident* or do not go to any trouble, do not inconvenience yourself: *Dinna fash yersel; you don't have to cook; we'll go out for a meal.*

faut fault: *It wis your faut.*

feart afraid: *The child's feart o' the dark.*

feartie, feardie a person who gets frightened easily, a coward: *The other kids said he was a feartie when he refused to fight.*

fecht fight, struggle: *two lads having a fecht in the playground.*

fechter fighter. A **bonnie fechter** someone who puts up a brave and determined struggle, often in the course of some kind of campaign: *We're protesting against the building of the new road and we've got some bonnie fechters on our side.*

ferlie *(now mostly literary)* something very strange: *People gathered to watch the ferlie in the sky.*

fermer farmer: *a sheep fermer.*

ferntickle a freckle: *She was a pretty red-haired, fair-skinned child with a face covered in ferntickles.*

fey *(now literary)* fated to die, doomed. People who were in this unfortunate position supposedly demonstrated exceptionally high spirits and this state was also referred to as **fey**.

fiddler, a fiddler's bidding/biddin' a last-minute invitation to a social occasion: *We've just got a fiddler's bidding to Anne's wedding next week and we're certainly not going to go.*

finnan haddie a smoked haddock. [From a method preparation first used in **Findon**, a village south of Aberdeen]

first foot 1. the person who is the first to enter a house at New Year. **2. first-foot** to be the first person to enter a house or visit its occupants at New Year: *I'm going round to first-foot my parents.* [Traditionally, the most popular first foot is a dark-haired man because he is thought to bring exceptionally good luck. It is thought to be very unlucky if a first foot arrives at your door empty-handed. At the very least, the first foot will be expected to have a bottle of whisky]

fit foot: *You stood on ma (=my) fit.*

fitba football: *the fitba season.*

flair floor: *washing the kitchen flair.*

flech flea: *The dug (=dog) must have flechs; he's scratching a lot.*

fleein' literally flying, but mostly now used to mean very drunk: *Tom and his friends were really fleein' at his stag night.*

fleg 1. a fright: *You gave me a real fleg by jumping out like that.* **2.** to frighten someone: *Stop shouting; you'll fleg the kids.*

flit to move house: *We're packing up, ready to flit on Friday.* **Flitting** the act of moving house.

flooer flower: *bluebells and ither (=other) flooers.*

fly cunning: *I'm sure Bill took the money, but he's too fly to get caught.*

flyte to scold or rail at: *His wife's a real nag and she's aye (=always) flyting at him.*

foosty mouldy, musty: *The sandwiches were two days old and had gone foosty.*

footer, fouter to fiddle: *The child just footered with his food and ate hardly anything.* **footerie, fouterie** used of a task that is rather fiddly and often involves manoeuvring small pieces: *Putting this toy together is a bit footerie.*

forby 1. besides, in addition: *He gets mair (=more) money in this job, and more time off forby.* 2. except: *I've got everything forby milk.*

forenoon the later part of the morning: *I'm working this forenoon, but I can meet you at lunch time.*

forfochen completely worn out, exhausted: *They were fair (=very) forfochen at the end of the journey.*

forkietail, forkie an earwig.

forrit, furrit forward: *Move furrit a bit.*

fou 1. full. 2. drunk: *He gets fou every Saturday.* [You can be as **fou as** various things, such as **fou as a wulk**, a **wulk** being a whelk]

fower four: *Fower were killed.*

fowk folk, people: *Fowk should mind their ain (=own) business.*

Free Church of Scotland *see* **Wee Free**.

frae *same as* **fae**.

freen friend: *The bairn's (=child's) made a new freen at school.*

furrit *same as* **forrit**.

fushionless lacking in energy, vigour or drive: *He's too fushionless to go out and find a job.*

fykie 1. difficult to please: *The child's too fykie about her food.* **2.** of a task, fiddly or intricate, requiring attention to detail: *Decorating this cake is a real fykie job.*

G

gae go: *Time will gae fast.* The past tense is **gaed**: *They gaed last week.*

gairden garden: *a gairden fou* (=full) *of weeds.*

gallus cheekily self-confident, cocky, daring: *Gallus young men showing off to their girlfriends.* [Although now often used to express admiration, however reluctant, the word originally was used in a more derogatory way, meaning wild, villainous or wicked and has associations with the word **gallows**, used for hanging]

galluses braces for holding up trousers: *He ran out wi* (=with) *his galluses dangling fae* (=from) *his troosers* (=trousers).

gang *(now less common than* **gae***)* go: *time to gang hame* (=home).

gar *(now mostly literary)* to make or cause someone to do something: *It wid* (=would) *gar ye greet* (=weep).

gate *(usually found in street names)* a way, road or street: *Canongate.* [If **ye gang yir ain gate** you literally go your own way and act in the way you want to do]

gaun 1. going: *Are ye gaun to work?* **2.** go on, found in the slang phrase **gaun yersel** used to express encouragement or approval to someone.

gaunie, gaunae, gauny going to: *Are ye gaunie make the tea?*; often used as a kind of request, *Gaunie help me wi this? Gaunie no shout*

(=Will you please not shout)?

gawkit 1. clumsy, awkward: *The gawkit teenager had become a lovely, poised young woman.* 2. stupid: *He was too gawkit to see that he was being conned.* [From **gawk**, a fool, a clumsy person]

gean a wild cherry, a wild cherry tree. [The word has connections with Old French **guigne**, a kind of cherry]

get to succeed in going somewhere, to be allowed to go somewhere: *I didn't get to the match; the boss wouldn't give me time off.*

gey *(can rhyme either with* **high** *or* **hay**) very, exceptionally: *He's gey ill.*

gie to give: *Will you gie me a lift?*; **gies** is short for **gie us**, give us: *Gies a drink.* The past tense is **gied**.

gigot a leg of lamb; a **gigot chop** is a lamb chop that has been taken from the leg of the animal. [From French **gigot**, a leg of lamb or mutton]

gin *(now mostly literary)* if: as in the popular Burns' song—*'gin a body meet a body* (=someone) *comin' through the rye'.*

ginger *(informal, especially used in West Central Scotland)* a fizzy soft drink of any flavour: *The kids wanted a drink of ginger.*

girdle a kind of strong, flat, round iron pan with a semi-circular handle, used for baking scones or pancakes on top of a cooker. It was originally used over an open fire, the handle being used to suspend it. **A girdle scone** is a scone which has been cooked on a girdle, rather than in an oven.

girn to complain, grumble or whine: *My neighbours are girning about* the noise and *The kids are girning about spending so long in the car.*

glaikit foolish, half-witted, silly: *The glaikit sales assistant gave me the wrong change.*

glaur soft sticky mud: *The kids were playing on the river bank in the pouring rain and they came home covered in glaur.*

gleg *(now mainly literary)* quick and agile, whether physically or mentally: *He's too gleg to be taken in by that trick.*

glen *(often used in place names)* a valley, usually quite narrow, between steep hills with a river running through it: *Glencoe.* A **strath** is the name given to a much wider valley: *Strathearn.*

gloaming *(usually now mainly literary)* twilight, dusk: *It was gloaming and farm workers were making for home.*

golach a beetle. [From Gaelic for an earwig, **gobhlag**; in Scots, an earwig is sometimes called a **horny golach**]

gomerel a stupid person, a fool: *Some gomerel's bought Jock's old wreck of a car.*

gowan a daisy or a marguerite.

gowk a fool, a simpleton: *You must think I'm a real gowk to be taken in by that trick.* [The word is sometimes used with reference to an **April fool**. A **gowk** originally meant a **cuckoo**]

gowpin extremely painful, throbbing: *He's got a hangover and his heid's (=head's) really gowpin.*

graip a large fork used for farming or gardening work: *digging up tatties (=potatoes) wi a graip.*

greet to weep, to cry: *The baby started to greet*. The past tense can be **gret** or **grat**. Someone who is said to be a **greetin face** always looks miserable or unhappy and complains a lot.

green *see* **back green**.

grosset a gooseberry.

grue if something **gars you grue** it fills you with horror: *Seeing those cruel instruments of torture gars me grue*. [**Grue** has obvious connections with the English word **gruesome**]

grun ground: *a drunk lying on the grun*.

gub 1. *(informal and usually used rather rudely)* the mouth: *Shut your gub!* 2. *(informal)* to defeat heavily: *We were meant to be the stronger team, but we got gubbed*.

guddle a mess or state of confusion: *I overslept this morning and I've been in a bit of a guddle all day*. [To **guddle** for fish is to try to catch the fish with your hands]

guising a Hallowe'en tradition by which children dress in fancy dress, often as characters associated with the festival, such as witches or ghosts. Then the **guisers** go round local houses performing short acts of entertainment and receiving small gifts of sweets, fruit or money.

guts to eat greedily. **gutsie, gutsy** greedy: *gutsie people helping themselves to huge portions*.

guttered one of several words in Scots meaning extremely drunk: *He comes home guttered every Saturday night*. [Likely to come from an association with a **gutter** in the street, into which a drunk might fall as he/she staggers home]

gutties gymshoes, plimsolls: *kids changing into gutties for their gym lesson*. [From **gutta percha**, a type of rubber]

H

haar a cold sea mist which drifts in from the North Sea along the east coast: *It was a lovely sunny day inland, but much of Edinburgh was covered in a haar*. [The word **haar** may be from a Dutch word meaning a bitterly cold wind and **haar**, in Scots, used to have the additional meaning of a cold east wind coming in from the North Sea]

hack a crack in the skin caused by cold: *Without gloves her hands were covered in hacks in winter*.

hackit ugly, unattractive: *Mary's lovely, but her sister is a big hackit, untidy woman*.

hae have: *I hae a message for you*.

hale, hail whole: *He was ill his hale life*.

hame home: *I wis (=was) ill and went hame early*.

hand if you **tak your hand off someone's face** you slap them.

handsel a gift given to someone at the start of something, intended to bring them good luck. To **handsel** someone is to give them such a gift, but it also means to celebrate the first use of something or to use something for the first time: *Let's handsel the new glasses by drinking some champagne*.

hap to cover: *plants happed with straw to protect them from frost*. If you **hap up** you cover yourself in warm clothing to protect yourself against the cold: *In this weather old people need to be well happed up*.

harl 1. to coat a wall with a mixture of lime and very small stones: *The builder is harling the garage*. 2. a mixture of lime and very small stones used in this way.

hash 1. to move about in a very hurried, flustered way: *There's no point in hashing up the hill; the bus has already left*. 2. to do something in a hurried, clumsy or inexpert way: *I don't want workmen hashing away at the building work; I want it done properly*.

haud hold: *Haud on, I'm just coming* and *Take haud o' this*.

hauf half: *He got hauf the money*. A **hauf** is a **half** and it is also used to refer to a small glass of whisky, originally half a gill. A **wee hauf** was originally a quarter of a gill.

haun 1. a hand: *a safe pair o' hauns*. 2. to hand someone something: *She haunded me the baby*.

haiver, haver to talk nonsense: *Jack's haverin when he says that he'll get the job*.

heavy a type of beer roughly equivalent to English bitter. **Heavy** is slightly weaker in strength and lighter in colour than **export**.

hee-haw *(informal)* mostly commonly used in West Central Scotland, means absolutely nothing: *He cares hee-haw for her*.

heid the head: *He's got a sair* (=sore) *heid*.

heidbanger *(informal)* someone who acts in a wild, crazy way: *The car was stolen by a heidbanger who drove into a wall*.

heid bummer *(informal)* someone in a position of authority, someone in charge of something: *He's heid bummer of the council now.*

heidie *(informal)* a head teacher: *The heidie's sent for the truants.*

hen a friendly term used in greeting a girl or woman: *Is this your bag, hen?*

hen-toed with the points of the feet turned inwards.

hert heart: *a warm hert.*

het hot: *a cup o' het tea.*

heukbone steak the equivalent of English **rump steak**.

high heid yin *(slang)* a person in a position of authority or power: *The factory workers are badly paid, but the high heid yins earn a fortune.*

high tea a meal traditionally consisting of a single savoury course, served with tea and an assortment of bread and cakes of the kind associated with afternoon tea, and eaten in the early evening. The meal is often now called just **tea**, although this can apply to the evening meal, whatever the content and whenever it is eaten.

hin-end the back of something, a person's backside or buttocks: *Get aff (=off) yer hin-end and get some work done.*

hing hang: *the rope hingin frae (=from) the ceiling.*

hirple to limp, to walk with great difficulty, to hobble: *She was hirpling along on ridiculously high heels.*

hoast cough: *patients in the doctor's waiting room sneezin and hoastin and a terrible smoker's hoast.*

Hogmanay the night of December 31, called in England New Year's

Eve and a time of celebration and revelry in Scotland.

hotchin, hoatchin very busy or crowded: *It was Christmas Eve and the shops were hotchin.* **hoatchin wi** to be full, to be swarming with, to be infested with: *The village was hotchin wi reporters* and *The cat's hotchin wi flees.*

hochmagandy *(now mostly literary or facetious)* sexual intercourse.

hoodie a crow, especially a hooded crow. [Not to be confused with the now English **hoodie**, meaning a kind of sweatshirt with a hood, often worn by male teenagers, and sometimes meaning also the wearer of this]

hooch the cry uttered by dancers when an energetic reel is in progress.

hoolet an owl: *I heard a hoolet screech.* [Another Scots word with a French origin, **houlotte**, an owl]

hoor a whore, also used as a general term of abuse for any woman.

hoose house: *the hoose next door.*

hough *see* **potted hough**.

howk to dig something up, to extract something with difficulty: *I'll need to howk these weeds up.* [See **tattie howkin'**.]

humph to carry something heavy: *We had to humph our luggage from the station to the hotel.*

hunkers the backs of the thigh. **sit on your hunkers** to squat down: *She sat on her hunkers and tried to comfort the little girl.*

hunner a hundred: *a hunner years*.

hurdies the buttocks, the haunches.

hurl a lift in a car etc: *The kids asked him for a hurl in his new car*.

I

ilk literally the same (place, thing, person etc), often used in a person's title to indicate that the person named is the owner or laird of the place named: *Sir Robert Erskine of that ilk, Erskine being a place*. [In English **of that ilk** has come to mean of that kind: *The resort has been ruined by rowdy teenagers and others of that ilk*]

ilka *(now mostly literary)* every, each: *ilka child knows*.

inby inside a house: *Mum's inby; I'll get her for you*.

ingin an onion: *steak and ingins*.

isnae is not: *Is he isnae here?*

ither other: *I like the ither yin (=one) better*.

J

jag a prick with something sharp, often used to mean an injection or vaccination: *The baby got his measles jag today*. **jag** also means to prick or pierce or to hurt yourself in this way: *I jagged my hand on that rusty nail*.

jaggy prickly or piercing, likely to sting: *jaggy nettles*.

jaicket jacket: *take aff (=off) his jaicket*.

jalouse *(now mostly literary)* to suspect: *I jaloused that he was the thief.*

jannie *(informal)* a school janitor.

janitor the person in charge of the maintenance and cleaning of a building, especially a school: *The janitor switched on the central heating.*

jaw-box a kitchen sink. [May have connections with **jaw**, an old Scots word for to splash, spill or pour]

jeelie jelly or jam: *a jeely jaur* (=jam jar). **jeelie piece** a jam sandwich.

jenny-a'-things a small shop that sells a wide range of different things: *I got the marble in the village jenny-a'-things when I was a bairn* (=child).

jessie an insulting term for a man who is considered to be effeminate, a cissy: *The big jessie's greetin because his wife's left him.*

jiggered completely worn out, exhausted: *I'm jiggered after that long drive.*

jiggin, the jiggin a dance, dancing: *Are ye going to the jiggin tonight?*

jing-bang, the hale/hail jing-bang the whole lot: *We sold the hale jing-bang at the car boot sale.*

jings! An exclamation of surprise: *Jings! Is that the time?*

joco happy, pleased with yourself: *Jean's quite joco because she's passed her driving test.* [A shortened form of English **jocose**]

jook *same as* **jouk**.

jorrie a marble: *kids playing a game of jorries.*

jotter a school exercise book: *Write the essay in your English jotter*. **get your jotters** *(informal)* to get the sack from your job: *You'll get your jotters if you're late again.*

jouk, jook to dodge or duck: *He nearly hit me on the nose but I jouked just in time* and *The policeman came after us, but we jouked down the side of the building and he lost us.*

K

kail, kale 1. a kind of cabbage. 2. a vegetable soup.

keech *(the ch is pronounced as in* **loch***)* excrement: *I stepped in some dog's keech.*

keek 1. to glance or peep at something: *I keeked through a chink in the curtains.* 2. a glance or peep.

keeker a black eye: *Tom's been in a fight; he's got a right keeker.*

keelie now often used to refer to Glaswegian (**Glesca keelie**), often in a derogatory way; originally used to refer to a rough working-class male city-dweller. [From Gaelic **gille**, a young man]

kelpie a water spirit in the shape of a horse. According to Scottish folklore, they tried to lure people to a watery grave in the lochs and rivers that they inhabited.

ken to know: *I ken his wife and I ken where he stays.* The word **ken** is used in the same way as English **you know** as a kind of meaningless sentence filler: *He's a hard worker, ken.*

kenspeckle easily recognized, familiar, conspicuous: *The old tramp was a kenspeckle figure in these parts.*

kirk church, especially a Presbyterian church. The Church of Scotland is sometimes referred to as **The Kirk**.

kist a large wooden box or chest: *The bed linen is kept in a kist in the hall.*

knock *(now rather old-fashioned or literary)* a clock: *the knock on the bedside table.*

kye cattle: *milking the kye.*

kyle *(mostly now found in place names)* a narrow strip of water: *Kyle of Lochalsh.*

L

laddie a boy, a youth: *The killer was just a laddie.*

lad o' pairts a clever boy, particularly one from a poor family who is likely to do well: *a lad o' pairts working to pay his university fees.*

laldie, gie it laldie to do something with great vigour: *The pianist fairly gied it laldie and everyone joined in the singsong.*

lane, on your lane by yourself: *Jock's been on his lane since his wife left.*

lang long: *lang summer days.*

lassie a girl or young woman: *He's marryng a lassie fae* (=from) *Perth.*

laverock the lark.

leet a list of candidates for a job. This **long leet** is whittled down to a **short leet**, a list of the candidates who are most likely to be in the running for the job.

len loan: *Can you len me a pen?* and *I got a len o' Jim's car.* If you **take a len of someone** you take advantage of them or impose on their good nature or naivety.

licht light: *by the licht o' the moon.*

line a written authorization of some kind: *a doctor's line* (=a note from a doctor indicating that you are off work suffering from some form of illness).

links 1. a stretch of sandy undulating ground, often with rough grass or other vegetation, near the sea shore. The name became applied to a golf course in such an area and this use is widely known outside Scotland. 2. sausages of the kind joined in a chain: *A pound of links, please.*

linn 1. a waterfall, found in such place names as *Linn of Dee.* 2. a deep narrow gorge. [From Old English **hlynn**, a torrent]

linn 2. a pool beneath a waterfall: *fishing in the linn.* [From Gaelic **linn** a pool]

lintie the linnet: *hear the lintie singing.*

lippen to trust someone, to depend on someone to do something: *You can lippen on Jock tae* (=to) *look after the bairns* (=children).

loch a lake: *Loch Earn.* [From Gaelic]

lochan a small loch.

long lie if you **have a long lie** you stay in bed later in the morning than you usually do: *It's Sunday and so I can have a long lie.*

loof *same as* **luif**.

loon *(used mainly in the north-east of Scotland)* a boy or youth. [Originally used as term of abuse]

Lorne sausage sausage meat sold in the form of square slices.

loss to lose something: *Dinna* (=Don't) *loss your temper.*

lowp, loup to jump or leap: *The dog louped over the dyke.*

lowpin', loupin' *(especially in the Glasgow area)* **1.** extremely sore, throbbing with pain: *I sprained my ankle and it's loupin'.* **2.** infested with, full of, busy: *The cat's lowpin' wi fleas* and *It was Saturday night and the pub was lowpin'.*

lowsin' time the time at which work finishes: *lowsin' time is six o'clock. See* **yokin' time**. [To **lowse** something is to loosen it or release it; **lowse** also means loose]

lug the ear: *She whispered something in his lug.*

luif, loof *(now mainly literary)* the palm of the hand.

lum a chimney: *The lum's needin swept.* [The expression **lang may your lum reek**, literally long may smoke come from your chimney, is used to wish someone a long and happy life]

M

ma my: *That's ma wife.* [There is much greater use of **ma** and **my** and also of the other possessive pronouns, such as **yir/your,** than there is in English as, *I'm going to my bed* and *Have you had your dinner?*]

mair more: *There's nae* (=no) *mair milk.*

mairrit, merrit married: *She's a mairrit woman now.*

maist most: *Maist village fowk* (=people) *shop here.*

mak make: *He'll mak trouble, for sure.*

mammy *(especially in West Central Scotland)* mummy.

man husband: *Jean's man's left her and the kids.*

manky dirty, grubby: *This tablecloth is manky.*

manse a house provided by the Church of Scotland for a parish minister.

masel myself: *Ah* (=I) *really enjoyed masel.*

mask to make, brew or infuse tea: *This tea's just freshly masked.*

maukit, mawkit extremely dirty, filthy: *The kid's claes* (=clothes) *were maukit.*

maun must: *He maun try harder.*

mavis the song thrush.

maw *(especially in West Central Scotland)* mother: *The bairn's* (child's) *greeting* (=crying) *for her maw.*

meat *(often pronounced to rhyme with fate and sometimes spelt mate)* in Scots, **meat** can refer to any kind of food, or food in general, not just the flesh of animals: *He's ill and aff (=off) his meat.*

meenit a minute: *Wait a meenit.*

melt (informal) to hit someone very hard: *Say that again and I'll melt you.*

mercat market: *mercat cross.*

messages, go/do the messages to do the household shopping: *I usually do the messages on Thursday evening.*

micht might in all its several English meanings: *He micht just win.*

michty me! an exclamation of surprise.

mickle in the well-known saying **many a mickle maks a muckle** mickle has to mean a small amount to make sense. Yet, it was originally an alternative from of **muckle**, a large amount.

midden a rubbish tip, used figuratively to refer to a dirty person, thing or place: *This flat's a midden!*

mince nonsense, rubbish: *I certainly won't give him the job; he was talking absolute mince.* **thick as mince** means very stupid: *He's bound to fail the exam; he's thick as mince.*

mind to remember something: *I mind when that block of flats was a church.*

mingin having a very nasty smell: *There was a piece of rotting meat in the kitchen and it was mingin.* It is now used more generally, particularly by young people, to refer to something or someone very unpleasant or of very poor quality: *I'm not living in that mingin flat and that's that.* [From the verb **ming** to have a very strong unpleasant smell]

mink a disreputable person, now used as a general term of abuse: *That mink sold me a dodgy car.* [From Gaelic **muince** a collar and, by extension, a noose: if this was a fate that a **mink** deserved]

mint imperial *same as* **pandrop.**

miraculous *(pronounced mir-rock-you-luss)* extremely drunk: *He was miraculous when he fell into the canal.*

mirk darkness, murk, night, twilight: *I didn't get a right look at him in the murk.*

miss, miss yourself to miss an opportunity to enjoy yourself by not being present at an occasion: *You missed yourself last night. The party was fantastic.*

missives when you buy a house in Scotland your solicitor exchanges **missives** or formal letters with the seller's solicitor which commit both parties to the sale at the price stated in the letter.

mither mother: *She's the mither o' twins.*

mixter-maxter a jumble, a confused or muddled state: *The book is a mixter-maxter of various genres.*

mochie of air or weather unpleasantly humid; damp and misty: *It was sunny inland, but mochie by the east coast.*

mony many: *We've known each other mony a long year.*

moo, mou mouth: *Keep your mou shut.*

moose a mouse: *a cat chasing a moose*.

moothie a mouth organ, a harmonica: *The lad played his moothie at the ceilidh*.

morn, **the morn** tomorrow: *I'll see you the morn*.

the morn's morn tomorrow morning: *She's due back the morn's morn*.

muckle 1. very large, great: *The field's full of muckle stanes* (=stones); a very large amount. 2. much: *They're no* (=not) *muckle use*.

mull a headland or narrow peninsula: *the Mull of Kintyre*.

N

nae 1. no: *He has nae money*. 2. not: *She'll nae be long*.

naebdy nobody: *Naebdy wis there*.

nane none: *I looked for milk, but there's nane*.

neb the nose: *Don't stick your neb intae* (=into) *my business*.

nebby, nebbie nosey, inquisitive: *nebby neeboors* (=neighbours).

ned a young hooligan or petty criminal: *The old man was set on by a bunch of neds*.

neeboor, neebur a neighbour: *ma* (=my) *next-door neeboor*.

neep a turnip, particularly a swede: *mashed neeps*.

next *(when applied to days or months)* the next but one. [This can cause great confusion. If it is, say, Friday and a Scot refers to next Monday they will very likely be referring not to the nearest Monday as would be the case in English, but to the Monday after that. A Scot is likely to refer to the English **next Monday** as **this Monday**. The issue is further complicated by the fact that the English use is now also quite common in Scotland. It is better to mention the actual date, when in doubt]

nicht night: *It was a dark nicht.* **the nicht** tonight: *She gets here the nicht.*

nieve the clenched fist: *shaking his nieve angrily at them.*

nippy sweetie *(informal)* a person, often a woman, who has a reputation for being sharp-tongued or easily annoyed: *My son's new teacher seems a right nippy sweetie.*

no not: *It's no rainin'.*

noo now: *It's winter noo.* **the noo** just now: *They're no (=not) in the noo.*

numpty a stupid or foolish person: *You were a right numpty to do that.*

nyaff a term of abuse used to someone you regard as objectionable or contemptible, often to someone who is physically small: *That wee nyaff is really getting on my nerves.*

o' of: *a cup o' tea* and *make a real mess o' that.*

och *(rhymes with loch)* **1.** an expression used to express various feelings: surprise, annoyance, impatience, disagreement, weariness, pain: *Och, there's nothing wrong with you.* **2.** used meaninglessly as a preface to any remark: *Och, he's the same as always.*

och aye often used humorously by non-Scots in supposed imitation of Scots when the **och** is pronounced to rhyme with **rock**; sometimes extended to **och aye the noo** (=just now), although this is not at all common among Scots.

ocht anything: *Dae ye ken ocht aboot it?* (=Do you know anything about it?) [Scots from of the English **aught**]

offie *(informal)* an off-licence: *We'll get some beer from the offie.*

ongoings goings-on, events, sometimes of a suspicious or wild nature: *The tabloids were full of the ongoings at the MP's mistress's flat.*

ony any: *Has he ony money?*

oor our: *oor bairns* (=children).

oose fluff, dust: *This room needs cleaned; there's oose under the bed.* **oosey** covered in fluff or dust. [From the plural of **oo**, a Scots word for wool]

oot out: *Mum's oot; she's at work.*

ootby, outby 1. not indoors or inside: *He's ootby in the shed havin' a smoke.* 2. outlying, being a short distance a way: *the farm buildings and the outby fields.*

orra 1. odd, strange, abnormal: *an orra object in the sky.* 2. disreputable, rough, coarse: *a bunch o' orra fowk camping in the field.* **orraman** an odd job man, a man employed to do occasional, unskilled work. [The origin of the word may be **ower a'** (=over all, everywhere)]

outwith outside, beyond: *outwith the terms of the contract* and *outwith the school's catchment area.*

ower 1. over: *jump ower the fence.* 2. excessively: *ower hot.*

oxter the inside of the upper arm, armpit: *The child was up to his oxters in mud*. A person **wi his heid under his oxter** is feeling depressed.

P

pairt 1. part: *sailing to foreign pairts*. **lad o' pairts** see **lad. 2.** to part: *He'll no* (=not) *pairt with ony* (=any) *money*.

pan, knock yir pan oot to tire yourself out by working extremely hard: *I knocked ma* (=my) *pan oot for that firm and then they made me redundant*.

pancake the Scots pancake is made of a similar batter to other pancakes, but it is thicker in consistency, contains a raising agent and is cooked on a **girdle**, often formerly called a **drop scone**.

pandrop a type of hard round white mint sweet: *sucking a pandrop*. Also called a **mint imperial**.

pan loaf 1. a type of loaf with a smooth light crust all over the loaf, rather than just on the top and bottom as a **plain** loaf does. **2.** in a posh, often pretentious, English-sounding accent: *to talk pan loaf*. [The **pan loaf** was originally baked in an individual baking tin and was more expensive than a **plain loaf**. This gave the loaf its association with a higher social class: **talk pan loaf**]

park an enclosed field: *the cows in the park*.

parkie the attendant in a public park: *The parkie tried to catch the stray dog*.

parritch porridge **auld claes and parritch** *see* **claes**.

partan a crab, especially the edible variety: *a partan salad*. **partan bree** crab soup.

pauchle, pochle 1. to steal, to embezzle: *sacked for pauchling money from the firm*. 2. to rig, fix the votes in an election, the figures in a result etc: *vote-counters accused of pauchling the votes in the local election*. 3. an instance of rigging or fixing something. [The word **pauchle** once referred to something quite legitimate, to something that a worker was allowed to take home from work as a perk; it originally meant a package]

paw father, dad: *Paw, can ah (=I) have some sweeties?*

pawkie, pawky of a sense of humour, dry and down-to-earth. [From **pawk** an old word for a crafty trick]

pech to breathe hard from exertion, to pant, to puff: *We weren't very fit and we were all peching at the end of the race.*

peedie same as **peerie**.

peelie-wallie, peely-wally very pale and sickly-looking: *She's had flu and she's looking very peelie-wallie.*

peenge to whine or complain: *The kids are peenging about having to stay inside.*

peenie, peeny an apron: *She wore a peenie to wash the dishes*. [Short for **pinafore**]

peep a tiny light or flame, the lowest level at which a gas flame can be at without going out, hence the phrase **put someone's gas at a peep** to cut someone down to size, to put someone in their place: *Jean's very pretentious, but Bill's mother will soon put her gas at a peep.*

peerie 1. a spinning top, often one turned by means of a string. **peerie heels** stiletto heels.

peerie, peedie 2. small, tiny: *a peerie bedsit*.

peever 1. the game of hopscotch: *girls playing peever in the playground*. 2. the flat stone used in the game.

peewit the lapwing.

pellock a porpoise.

pend *(mostly now used in place names)* an arched passageway, often one running through a building into a courtyard behind it: *St Margaret's Pend*. [Originally an arch or vault and probably having connections with Latin **pendere,** to hang]

perjink smart, neat sometimes to the point of being fussy or over-precise: *She's so perjink about her appearance you never see her without make-up and her best clothes*.

petted lip a lower lip protruding in front of the upper lip, a sign of a sulk and often regarded as a sign of a spoilt child: *Look at that petted lip; she just wants her own way*.

petticoat tails triangular shortbread biscuits cut from a round. [Possibly from the fact that the outer edge of the dough is scalloped so that it resembles the hem of a petticoat; alternatively there is a theory that the pieces of shortbread were of French origin and were originally called **petites galettes,** being introduced from France by Mary Queen of Scots]

pickle, puckle a fairly small quantity or number of something, the 'of' being often omitted: *a pickle snow* and *a pickle books*. [Originally

pickle referred to a grain of corn]

piece a sandwich, often eaten as part of a packed lunch or as a snack: *The child wants a jeely piece* (=jam sandwich).

pinkie the small finger. [Several parts of America have this meaning; connected with Dutch **pink**, a little finger]

pirn a reel or bobbin for holding thread.

pish piss in its various meanings: **pished** extremely drunk, and **it's pishing down** it's raining very hard.

pit put: *We pit it there*.

plain loaf *see* **pan loaf**.

plank 1. to put something away for later use, to hide something: *The robbers planked the money before the police could find it*. 2. to put something down in a forceful or decisive manner: *She planked the 'missing' documents down in front of her boss*.

playpiece a snack taken to school by a child to be eaten during break or interval: *Her playpiece consisted of a packet of crisps and an orange*. [The snack would have originally been a **piece** or sandwich; *see* **piece**]

play yourself to play about, to amuse yourself, to mess about, wasting time: *Don't play yourself; you should be studying*.

pled pleaded: *In a court of law, he pled guilty*.

plook, plouk a pimple, spot or boil: *There's a red plook on my nose*.

plowter, plouter 1. to splash about or play about in water: *kids plowtering about in puddles*. 2. to mess about, to potter about, to do something in an aimless way: *Stop plowtering about and get some studying done.*

plunk, plunk school to play truant: *He was suspended for plunking school.*

poind of the officers of a court, to take possession of the goods of a debtor with the intention of selling them in a **warrant sale** if the debts are not paid, the proceeds of the warrant sale being put towards the repayment of the debts.

poke a bag, especially a small paper one: *a poke o' sweeties.*

pokey-hat an ice cream cone. [From the cone's resemblance to a (long, pointed) hat]

policies the enclosed parkland and gardens surrounding a large house: *the large Georgian house and its extensive policies.*

polis *(pronounced as po-lis)* **1.** police: *There was a fight at the pub and the polis were sent for.* **2.** a policeman: *There's a polis at the door.*

pooch pocket: *Ma (=My) wallet was in ma back pooch.*

pope's eye steak a cut of rump steak for frying or grilling.

potato scone *same as* **tattie scone**.

potted heid, pottit heid a dish made from the head of a cow or pig which has been boiled, chopped or shredded, and covered in jelly made from the stock, eaten cold.

potted hough, pottit hough a dish similar to **potted heid**, but made from the **hough** or shin of a cow or pig.

pou, pu pull: *The horse'll pou the cairt* (=cart) *and Pou some roses.*

pow *(rhymes with cow)* the head or the skull: *But blessings on your frosty pow,* a line from Burns' song *John Anderson, My Jo.*

preen a metal pin: *putting preens in the hem of the skirt.*

press a large cupboard, often a built-in one: *The raincoats are in the hall press.*

price if something **is the price of someone** it means that is what that person deserves, that it serves them right: *It'll be the price of you if the police catch you.*

procurator fiscal *(often abbreviated to* **fiscal***)* a legal official in an area, appointed by the Lord Advocate, who acts as prosecutor for the crown. It is his/her job to decide whether there is enough evidence against someone for a criminal trial to be held and to decide whether there has been any illegal circumstances, such as murder, surrounding a sudden death: *A report has been sent to the procurator fiscal.*

provost until 1975, the name given to the head of the town council in Scottish burghs. **Lord Provost** a courtesy tile given to the chairperson of the councils of certain Scottish cities, such as Edinburgh and Glasgow.

public school a former term for a school run by a local education authority. [A completely different meaning from the **English public school**]

puckle *same as* **pickle**.

puddock a frog or toad: *The kids are collecting puddock spawn.*

puggled 1. completely exhausted: *I've been on night shift and I'm puggled.* **2.** drunk.

puir poor: *puir fowk* (=people) *in need o' money for food* and *The puir lad's really ill.*

pulley an indoor frame, consisting of long horizontal bars, for hanging clothes on. It is suspended from the ceiling of a room, usually the kitchen, and raised and lowered on a system of pulleys by a rope: *Now that I have a tumble drier I don't use my pulley so much.*

pump to break wind, to fart: *The child laughed in embarrassment and said, 'I pumped'.*

pun a pound: *a pun o' mince.*

pure in West Central Scotland, used before an adjective to indicate the greatest degree possible: *That's pure brilliant.*

Q

quaich *(the ch is pronounced as in loch)* a wide, shallow, bowl-like drinking vessel, often with a handle at each side; now mostly used as an ornament or trophy: *He was given a silver quaich as an eighteenth birthday present.* [From Gaelic **cuath**, a cup or bowl]

quair *(literary; mostly found in the titles of literary works)* a book: *A Scots Quair.*

queer great, substantial, considerable: *There's been a queer difference between house prices here and house prices in the city.*

quine *(in North East Scotland)* a girl, a young unmarried woman: *the quine that's engaged to Bill*. [A variant form of the obsolete word **quean**]

R

ra *(especially in West Central Scotland)* the: *Whaur's ra dug* (=dog)?

radge, sometimes **raj 1.** wild, crazy. **go radge** act in a wild, crazy manner, go mad: *Dad went radge when I crashed his car.* **2.** a wild character, a person who behaves in a wild, reckless way: *That wee radge caused a row in the pub last night.*

rag, lose your rag to lose your temper: *Jim doesn't often lose his rag, but he was furious at Tom last night.*

ragnail a hangnail, a loose piece of skin beside a finger nail: *This ragnail is sore.*

rammy a brawl, a free-for-all: *There was a rammy in the pub last night and the police were sent for.*

ramstam in a hurried, unrestrained, and often rather reckless, way: *The builders went at the house ramstam and finished it in time, but they made a lot of mistakes.*

randan if you **go on the randan** you go on some kind of spree, often a drinking binge: *Joe went on the randan last night and has a terrible hangover this morning.*

rasp a raspberry.

rax 1. to stretch: *He raxed out his hand and shook mine.* **2.** to sprain (a wrist, ankle, etc): *I tripped and raxed my ankle.*

rector 1. a university official elected by students to represent their interests: *Who is rector of Aberdeen University?* **2.** in some secondary schools, the headteacher: *the rector of Morrison's Academy*.

redd to clean or tidy up something: *redd the table after tea*. **redd up** to clean or tidy up: *I'll just redd up in here before I go*.

reek 1. smoke: *the reek from the wood fire*. **2.** of a chimney, etc. to smoke: *It was winter and the lums were reekin' all over the town*.

reset the criminal act of receiving stolen goods, knowing them to be stolen and often intending to resell them: *The antique dealer has just been charged with reset*.

richt right: *He had nae* (=no) *richt sayin' that* and *Turn richt here* and *He's richt handsome*.

rickle a loosely put together heap or pile of things, now often found in the phrase **a rickle o' banes**. See **bane**.

rift belch: *He gave a loud rift after the meal* and *He embarrassed her by rifting loudly*.

rin run: *Rin for your life*.

rodden the rowan berry; the rowan tree.

roon round: *go roon and roon*.

round steak a cut of beef taken from the hindquarters of the animal.

roup a public auction: *He went bankrupt and his belongings were put up for sale by public roup*. [From an earlier meaning of **roup**, to call or shout, the connection being that a **roup** was once publicly announced by proclamation]

rowan the mountain ash.

rowie a kind of flaky morning roll made with a great deal of butter, originating in North East Scotland. Also known as a **butterie/buttery rowie** or simply a **butterie/buttery**.

rummle 1. rumble: *the rummle o' thunder.* **2.** to move about noisily: *He came in late and rummled around the place waking everybody up.* **rummle up** to handle roughly, to beat: *rugby players trying to rummle up the opposition.*

runkle to crease or crumple something: *Sitting all day had runkled her linen skirt.* **runkled** creased or crumpled: *I need to iron this runkled blouse.*

S

sae so: *He's no* (=not) *sae daft as to believe that.*

saft soft: *saft tae* (=to) *the touch* and *She's tae* (=too) *saft wi her kids* and *He's saft in the heid* (=head).

sair 1. sore: *a sair heid* (=head). **it's a sair fecht** life is a great struggle. **2.** very much, greatly: *sair upset.*

sang song: *the auld Scots sangs.*

sannie a plimsoll, a gym shoe: *It's gym today and I'll need my sannies.* [Short for **sandshoe**]

sapsy 1. weak-willed, unable to stand up for yourself: *Stop being so sapsy and tell him to get lost.* **2.** over-sentimental, sloppy: *singing sapsy songs.*

sark *(now slightly old-fashioned)* a man's shirt; formerly also a woman's chemise: mentioned in Burns' narrative poem *Tam o' Shanter* when

Tam referred to the youngest witch as *Cutty Sark* because of the short chemise she was wearing.

Sassenach *(usually used humorously)* an English person. [Originally the word also applied to a lowland Scot as well; from Gaelic **Sassunach**]

sax six: *sax o'clock*.

scart to scratch or scrape: *She scarted his face wi* (=with) *her nails*. [A form of English **scrat**, later **scratch**]

scheme *(short for **housing scheme**)* a housing estate, especially one composed of houses built by a local authority: *All the trouble's being blamed on the kids from the scheme*. [Originally the plan drawn up for the building of a local authority housing estate]

sclim, sklim to climb: *sclim the cliff*.

scone *(in Scots **scone** rhymes with **gone** although in English it rhymes with **bone**)* Scones were originally cooked on a **girdle**, although they are now usually cooked in an oven. **Who stole your scone?** Why are you looking so miserable?

scoor to scour, to clean by energetic scrubbing: *scoor the porridge pan*.
scoor-oot the scattering of coins at a wedding for children to pick up, the practice being formerly quite common.

scoosh *same as **skoosh**.

scud 1. a slap, a smack: *She was angry and gave the kid a scud*.

scud, in the scud 2. naked: *She answered the door in the scud*.

scunner 1. to disgust, to cause dislike in: *His attitude towards women really scunners me*. **2.** a feeling of disgust or dislike: *I've taken a real* *scunner to meat*. **3.** someone or something who makes you feel disgust or dislike: *It's a right scunner that I'm going to have to miss the match*.

scutter to do something in a messy, careless way. **scutter about** to fiddle about, to spend time in pointless, time-wasting things: *Stop scuttering about and do some studying*.

see used to introduce a reference to a person or a thing to be discussed: *See him; he's a crook*. **see's** give me/us, hand me/us: *See's that paper ower* (=over).

seen, I've seen me a reference to the fact that you have done something in the past: *I've seen me rushing out to buy his books in hardback*.

seevin seven: *seevin days*.

sel self, used in compounds: *masel* (=myself), *hersel* (=herself): *He went by himsel* (sometimes hissel).

selkie a seal: *selkies basking on a rock*.

selt sold: *He selt me this car*.

semmit, simmit an undershirt, a vest, often originally made of flannel or wool: *It's too warm to wear a semmit*.

shauchle to walk slowly in an awkward, shambling way, to shuffle: *The old man shauchled doon* (=down) *the street in his slippers*. **Shauchlin, shauchlie** unsteady on your feet, shuffling.

shaw 1. the leaves and stalks of some root vegetables: potatoes and turnips: *tattie shaws*. **2.** to remove the stalks and leaves from a root vegetable. [The word **shaw** was Scots for **show** and **shaws** are the part of the plant that can be seen above ground]

shed a parting in the hair: *Her hair has a shed down the middle.*

sheltie a Shetland pony: *learning to ride on a Sheltie.*

shenachie a teller of traditional Gaelic stories; originally a recorder of family or clan history.

sherrakin, shirrakin a public scolding or rebuke: *The truants got a real sherrakin from the teacher.*

shilpit very thin and weak-looking as though suffering from malnutrition: *Tom was a shilpit creature until he stopped smoking and started eating properly.*

shoogle to shake, to rock from side to side: *The table shoogled and the drinks spilt.* **shoogly, shooglie** unsteady, shaky, wobbly: *I nearly fell off that shoogly chair.*

shoon shoes: *a pair o' satin dancin' shoon.*

shoother shoulder: *carry the load on his shoothers.*

shot 1. a turn: *You've been playing pool for ages; it's our shot now.* 2. the temporary use of something: *Can I have a shot on your new computer?*

shoulder steak English chuck steak.

shows a funfair with rides, such as roundabouts, and sideshows: *The kids went on the dodgems at the shows.*

sic such: *I felt like sic a fool.*

sicht sight: *a sicht for sore eyes.*

sicker, siccar sure: *I'll mak siccar.*

sideyways, sidieways sideways: *The crab moves sideyways.*

siller 1. silver: *a siller cup.* 2. money: *That's a lot o' siller for a bike.*

simmit *same as* **semmit**.

single end a one-room dwelling place, usually a tenement flat: *They brought up two kids in a single end.*

skail 1. to spill: *Watch out; you'll skail the beer.* 2. of a building, to empty out: *The church usually skails at half-past eleven.* 3. of people, to leave a building at the end of an event, to disperse: *Workers skailing from the factory at closing time.*

skean-dhu *(pronounced **skee**-an-doo)* a kind of short dagger with a black hilt, worn at the top of the right sock as part of a man's formal Highland dress. [From Gaelic **sgian-dubh**, a black knife]

skeich in high spirits, excited: *The kids are always skeich on Christmas morning.*

skeerie flighty, skittish: *The girls had had quite a lot to drink and were a bit skeerie.* [From **skeer** Scots from of **scare**]

skelf 1. a splinter of wood: *I've got a skelf in my finger and it's sore.* 2. someone who is very small and thin: *She's a wee skelf o' a woman, but she can carry really heavy weights.*

skellie squint. **skellie-eyed** having a squint.

skelp a smack, a slap: *If you're cheeky again I'll gie (=give) you a skelp.*

skinnymalink an extremely thin person or animal.

skint a **skint** knee is a grazed knee. [Scots form of **skinned**]

skirl a loud shrill sound, often used with reference to the sound of the bagpipes.

skirlie a dish made of onions and oatmeal fried together.

skite 1. a glancing blow: *He gave the boy a skite on the ear.* **2.** to bounce off something: *The hailstones skited off the car roof.* **3.** to slip or slide on something: *I skited on the ice and broke my ankle.*

skitter, skitter about to potter about, to waste time doing trivial things: *Stop skittering about and get ready for school.*

skitters a bout of diarrhoea.

skoosh, scoosh 1. to squirt, to gush in spurts: *Water was skooshing out of the fountain.* **2.** a squirt: *a skoosh of soda in the whisky.*

slabber to produce a lot of saliva, often in the course of eating: *the dog slabbering over a bone.* [Scots form of **slobber**]

slainte mhath (*pronounced slan-ja-vah*) good health, cheers; a Gaelic toast now fairly common throughout Scotland, and often shortened to **slainte**.

slaister 1. to make a mess, especially with something liquid or semi-liquid: *The child's not painting; she's just slaistering.* **2.** a mess, especially a wet, sloppy one. **3.** a messy person or eater.

slater a woodlouse.

sleekit untrustworthy and sly: *The old woman thinks he's charming, but he's sleekit; he's after her money.*

slider a portion of ice cream between two wafers.

slitter 1. to make a mess, especially with something liquid, or semi-liquid: *The kids are slittering about with the watering can.* 2. a sloppy mess. 3. a messy person, eater or drinker.

sma hoors the earliest hours of the morning: *It was the sma hoors before the train got there.* [**Sma** means small; the phrase has been adopted into English and often becomes **the wee sma hoors**, although **wee**, small, is redundant]

smeddum mettle, drive, resourcefulness, accompanied by common sense: *He doesn't have the smeddum to run a successful business.* [Originally a fine powder used in baking or as a medicine]

smirr a fine rain, a drizzle: *It's only a smirr; we can still have the picnic.*

smit, get the smit to become infected with an infection or disease: *I've got a bad cold; I must have got the smit from Jean.*

smoor to suffocate: *deliberately smoored wi* (=with) *a pillow.*

smowt, smout a very small person, a small child: *She was just a wee smout when her mother died.* [Originally a young salmon or sea trout]

snaw snow: *drifting snaw.*

sneck a catch or latch on a door or gate, of the type that is lifted by raising a small lever: *put the sneck on the door.*

snell bitterly cold: *It's a snell morning; it looks like snow.*

snib a bolt or catch on a door, for example: *Yale locks have a snib that can be put down for greater security.*

sodger soldier: *sodgers marching to war.*

sonsie plump and attractive-looking, made well-known by Burns when he addressed the haggis in his poem *To a Haggis*—'*Fair fa' your honest sonsie face.*'

soor sour. **soor ploom** a type of round green boiled sweet tasting rather tart.

sort 1. to put in good order, to tidy: *Sort your hair before you go to school*. **2.** to mend or fix: *Can you sort the car?*

sot so, used, mostly by children, to contradict a negative statement: '*You don't have a computer.*' '*I do sot!*'

souch of the wind, to blow with a murmuring or rushing sound: *a cold wind souching down the valley*. [If you **keep a calm souch** you remain calm and tranquil and do not panic]

spail a splinter, a chip or sliver of wood: *a spail in his bare foot*.

speir to ask, to inquire: *He speirt her name*.

speug (pronounced **spyug**), **spug** a sparrow.

split new brand new: *I got these shoes in a charity shop, but they're split new*.

spurtle a wooden stick used for stirring porridge.

squeegee askew, at the wrong angle: *That picture's squeegee; I'll straighten it*.

stair often used in Scots instead of **stairs**. **up/doon the stair** upstairs/downstairs.

stairheid a landing at the top of a flight of stairs, especially stairs in a tenement building.

stance 1. a bus terminus, a bay in a bus station where a bus stands.
2. a place where taxis wait for customers.

stank a gutter, a drain in the street; the grating over a drain: *Her ring fell doon* (=down) *the stank*. [If something is **doon the stank** it is lost forever: *money doon the stank*]

stappit, stappit fou extremely full, full as possible: *The shops were stappit fou*.

stave to sprain: *I fell and staveded my wrist*.

stay, stey to live or have your home somewhere: *They now stay in the city*. [This Scots meaning of **stay** can cause confusion]

steamie a public wash-house. [If you're **the talk of the steamie** people are gossiping about you]

steamin' one of several Scots words meaning extremely drunk: *absolutely steamin'*.

still and on nevertheless: *He's quite ill; still and on, he's lucky to be alive*.

stoat *same as* **stot**.

stoater something exceptional, a very attractive person, especially a girl or woman: *The new secretary's a real stoater*.

stotious extremely drunk: *He got absolutely stotious at the party last night*.

stookie a plaster cast: *His leg's in stookie*. [From **stucco**, plaster of Paris]

stoor, stour dust: *sweep up the stour from the cellar floor*. [It originally

67

meant a conflict or contest]

stooshie, stushie an uproar, a noisy protest: *create a stooshie about the new road*.

stot, stoat to bounce: *stot a ball*.

stottin', stoatin' so drunk that the person staggers or stumbles a lot.

stound, stoun, stoon 1. a stab of pain 2. to throb: *Ma (=My) tooth is stoundin'*.

stovies a traditional dish of sliced potatoes and onions.

stowed, stowed out extremely crowded, over-full: *The hall was stowed*.

stramash a noisy commotion, an uproar: *There was a real stramash when the pop concert was cancelled*.

strath *see* **glen**.

straucht, stracht, strecht straight: *a straucht line*.

stravaig to wander aimlessly, to roam: *stravaiging along the road, mindless of the traffic*. [From Latin **extravagare**, to wander]

sumph a stupid, useless person: *That sumph of a mechanic wrecked my car*.

swally 1. to swallow: *swally the pill*. 2. *(informal)* a drink of alcohol: *Comin' for a quick swally?*

sweetie a sweet: *sucking a sweetie*. [To **work for sweeties** is to work for very little money]

sweir reluctant or unwilling: *sweir to tell them the truth*. [It also once meant lazy, idle]

swither to be undecided as to which thing or course of action to chose: *I swithered between going on Saturday and going on Sunday.*

syboe, sybie a spring onion: *a salad with cucumbers and syboes*. [From French **ciboule**, an onion]

synd, syne to rinse something, to give something a quick wash: *I'll just synd oot* (=out) *this cup*.

syne since, ago. **lang syne** long since, long ago. [Known worldwide because of Burns' famous song *Auld Lang Syne*]

syver **1.** a drain or street gutter. **2.** the opening of a drain or the grating covering it: *He dropped his car keys down the syver.*

T

tablet a type of sweet, similar to fudge, but harder, made from butter, sugar and condensed milk. It is hardened in a flat oblong dish and cut into pieces, perhaps the origin of the word.

tackety boots boots with **tackets** (=hobnails or studs).

tae **1.** to: *I'm away tae bed*. **2.** too, as well: *She's bonny and she's brainy, tae*. **3.** the toe: *Ah've* (=I've) *hurt ma* (=my) *tae*.

tait a small amount of something, often **wee** tait: *a wee tait o' sugar in ma tea, please*.

tak take: *Tak care*.

Tam o' Shanter a man's round, flat brimless woollen cap, with a bobble on top, resembling a beret in style. [Named after the central character in Burns' poem *Tam o' Shanter*]

tap top: *the tap o' the hill and the tap o' the class.*

tapsalteerie upside down: *turn tapsalteerie.* [Scots form of **topsy turvy**]

tarry-fingered liable to steal things: *Don't leave your jewellery around when that odd-job man's around; people say he's tarry-fingered.*

tattie a potato: *tattie soup.*

tattie-bogle a scarecrow. *See* **bogle.**

tattie howkin' the harvesting of potatoes by digging them out of the ground and picking them up. *See* **howk.** [Traditionally schoolchildren in rural areas, in October, were given a holiday from school, known as **tattie holidays,** to help with the **tattie howkin'** and the October mid-term break is still sometimes known as **tattie holidays**]

tattie scone potato scone, a type of thin scone made from potato, flour and fat and cooked on a **girdle.**

tawse *same as* **belt.**

telling a warning, a lesson. **not to take a telling** to ignore a warning.

telt told: *Ah telt you no tae dae that* (=I told you not to do that).

tenement 1. a large building, usually of three or more storeys, divided into flats, each occupied by a different owner or tenant. 2. the section of such a building containing flats that are reached by a common stair and entered by a common **close.**

tent, tak tent *(now often literary)* to pay attention, to take care: *Let Wives Tak Tent*, the title of Robert Kemp's translation into Scots of Molière's play *L'Ecole des Femmes*.

teuchter *(often used in a derogatory manner)* **1.** a Lowland name for a Highlander, especially a Gaelic-speaking one. **2.** a country person: *It was market day and the town was full of teuchters*.

thae those: *Pass me thae books*.

the is often used in Scots with periods of time: *the day* (=today), *the morn* (=tomorrow).

thegither together: *tied thegither*.

thirled 1. so bound to a particular way of behaving, thinking or feeling that you do not even consider an alternative approach: *He's so thirled to eating meat and two veg that he won't try anything else*. **2.** bound to something from feelings of duty or obligation: *She was too thirled to the family firm to think of leaving the town*. [One of those invaluable Scots words which has no effective translation; shares an Old English origin with the English **thrall**]

thocht thought: *I thocht he had gone* and *hae* (=have) *gloomy thochts*.

thole to endure something, to put up with something: *The painkillers make me sick and so I'll just have to thole the pain* and *I can't thole my new boss*.

thon that, those: *thon black car in the garage*. [A combination of **that** and **yon**]

thrang 1. crowded: *pubs thrang wi football fans*. **2.** (of a person) busy or occupied: *It's harvest time and he's unco* (=very) *thrang*.

thrapple the throat or windpipe: *He took him by the thrapple and nearly choked him.* [Perhaps from Old English **throtbolla**, the Adam's apple]

thunderplump a sudden thundery shower of rain: *We got soaked in a thunderplump.*

ticht tight: *troosers* (=trousers) *that are too ticht.*

tig a children's game in which one player chases the others until he/she touches one of them. The person touched then does the chasing. [The equivalent of English **tag**]

tinker a member of travelling people who moves around the country doing casual work and selling and buying things: *I bought some clothes pegs from a tinker.*

tink 1. *(sometimes derogatory)* a tinker. **2.** used to refer to a mischievous child: *That wee tink won't go to sleep* and also used as a derogatory term for a person, especially a quarrelsome, vulgar or abusive person.

tirl to knock on something, to rattle something: *tirlin' at the windaes* (=windows) from the nursery rhyme *Wee Willie Winkie.*

tocher a marriage dowry, especially a bride's: *He married a lassie* (=girl) *with a substantial tocher.*

toom, tume empty: *a toom wallet.*

toon town: *the big shops in the toon.*

totie very small: *totie wee helpings.* [From **tot** meaning a small child, originally a Scots word]

tousie of hair, tangled and untidy: *combing the bairn's* (=child's) *tousie hair.* [From the same root as the English **tousle**]

trauchle 1. to walk, move or work slowly and wearily: *They trauchled up Station Hill, carrying their heavy suitcases*. 2. a tiring, monotonous task: *She finds waitressing a trauchle*. **trauchled** exhausted from being overburdened, overworked, etc: *trauchled mothers pushing pushchairs and carrying heavy bags from the supermarket*.

trews close-fitting tartan trousers worn by members of certain Scottish regiments as part of their formal uniform, and, by some as part of the formal Highland dress. [From the Gaelic **triubhas** trousers or trews]

tron (*mostly now found in place names:* **the Tron Kirk**) the place or building which, historically, housed the official public weighing machine in a town. [Originally the weighing machine itself]

tummle tumble. **tummle yir wulkies** *see* **wilkies**.

tumshie 1. a turnip. 2. a stupid person: *You tumshie, you've spilt my drink!*

twa two: *twa dugs* (=dogs).

twal twelve: *twal months*.

U

unco extremely, very: *an unco strange experience*. **the unco guid** is used to refer to people who are excessively self-righteous and often narrow-minded: *The young single mother has received much criticism from the unco guid in the community*. Robert Burns was one of the first to use this expression in his satirical poem *Address to the Unco Guid*. [A Scots variant of the English word **uncouth**]

uplift to collect or pick up: *You can uplift the goods directly from our warehouse*.

upset price the minimum price that a seller will accept in respect of the sale of something; formerly commonly used with regard to the sale of property, but nowadays the phrase **offers over** has replaced **upset price** in property adverts. [This is the equivalent of the English **reserve price**]

upstanding, be upstanding *(formal)*: *I would ask you all to be upstanding and drink a toast to Her Majesty the Queen.*

ur are: *We ur fed up.* **urnae**, are not: *We urnae sure.*

V

vennel *(often found in street names)* a lane or alley, often between houses: *King's Vennel.* [One of several words that have come into English from French; see note at **ashet**]

W

wa wall: *a brick wa.* [See note at **a'**]

wabbit *(also **wabbit oot**)* completely exhausted, tired out: *I'm fair wabbit oot after coming up that hill.*

wait on to wait for: *Don't wait on me; I'm not ready yet.*

wallie made of porcelain, china, or glazed earthenware: **wallie dug**, one of a pair of ornamental dogs made of porcelain placed at either end of a mantelpiece, formerly very popular, and **wallie close**, an entrance passageway to a **tenement** with walls covered in porcelain, china or glazed earthenware tiles. [The word **wallie** meant very fine and pleasant to look at before acquiring its meaning of ornamental]

wallies false teeth, dentures: *Granpa's taken oot* (=out) *his wallies.* [False teeth were once made of porcelain; see **wally**]

wame the stomach: *a sair* (=sore) *wame.* [A Scots form of **womb**]

wan one: *He's only got wan leg.*

wance once: *Ah* (=I) *wance kent* (=knew) *him.*

warrant sale a sale of goods belonging to a debtor authorized by a court: *Some essential household goods can be withheld from a warrant sale.*

waste **1.** to damage or spoil: *You'll waste yir* (=your) *good shoes if you walk in the puddles.* **2.** to spoil, over-indulge or pamper: *His granny wastes that child.*

watter water: *a cup o' watter.* [*See* **doon the watter** at **doon**]

wauchle to walk with great difficulty and often in an ungainly, stumbling manner: *Jean's pregnant wi* (=with) *twins and she can hardly wauchle doon* (=down) *the road.*

waukrife *(often now literary)* unable to sleep, sleepless: *spend a waukrife night thinking about his troubles.*

waur worse: *Things'll get waur before they get better.*

wean *(mostly in West Central Scotland)* a child: *She's only got wan* (=one) *wean.* [In other parts of Scotland the word for a child is **bairn**]

wee **1.** small, little: *I'm looking for a wee flat.* **2.** young, younger: *Her mother died when she was wee.* **a wee bit** slightly: *She's a wee bit sad.* [This word is one of Scotland's major linguistic contributions to the English language where it is quite common; it comes from an old English word for a weight]

Wee Free *(informal and sometimes rather derogatory)* a member of the Free Church of Scotland. [In 1843 the Free Church of Scotland broke away from the Church of Scotland, an event called the **Disruption**. A degree of reunion and reconciliation took place early in the twentieth century, but a minority of people rejected this reunion and reconciliation and continued to call themselves the **Free Church of Scotland**. The word **Wee** came to be associated with it because it has relatively few members, most of whom live in the West Highlands and the Hebrides]

wee hauf *see* **hauf**.

wee heavy a kind of strong beer, traditionally sold in smaller bottles or measures because of its strength.

weel well: *She's no* (=not) *weel* and *He plays weel* and *They're weel-kent* (=well-known) *here*.

wellied *(informal)* one of the many words in Scots for drunk: *It's Friday night and we're going to get wellied*.

well on drunk, well-advanced in the process of getting drunk: *The lads were well on when I left the pub*.

weemen women: *weemen workers*.

weird fate, destiny, now mostly found in the phrase **dree your weird** (*see* **dree**).

wersh 1. sour, bitter: *a cheap wersh wine*. 2. bland, insipid, lacking in flavour: *fish with a white wersh sauce*. [The first of these senses is now the more common, the second being the older, original meaning. With two such opposing senses the word can cause confusion, although neither sense is a compliment to the chef]

wha, whae who: *Wha's he?*

what used before adjectives in some exclamations: *What impertinence!* and *What interesting!*

what way 1. how, in what manner: *What way did he die?* **2.** why, for what reason: *What way did you say no?*

whaup a curlew.

whaur where: *Whaur's he fae?* (=Where's he from?)

wheech *(ch is pronounced as in* **loch***)* **1.** to move very quickly: *The biker wheeched away when he saw the policeman.* **2.** to move something away very quickly and suddenly: *My glass was wheeched away before I'd finished my wine.* **3.** a quick sudden movement: *We heard the wheech of the whip as he hit the poor animal.*

wheen, a wheen o' a few of, several, a fair number of: *a wheen o' jobs.*

wheesht! Be quiet! Shut up! **haud yir wheesht** to be quiet, to shut up: *Haud yir wheesht! Ah'm* (=I'm) *trying to hear what she's saying.*

whigmaleerie a decoration, an ornament, a trinket: *a funny old shop selling a lot of whigmaleeries.*

whiles sometimes, occasionally: *Whiles he's cheerful and whiles he's sad.*

whin gorse: *The whin was in bloom.*

whit what: *Whit went wrang* (=wrong)?

whit wey *same as* **what way**.

whitterick a weasel, a stoat.

wi with: *Come wi me.*

wid would: *I wid walk.*

widna, widnae wouldn't: *I widna dare.*

widdershins anti-clockwise; in the opposite direction to the usual one. Doing something **widdershins** is thought by some to bring bad luck or evil and, traditionally, witches are said to dance **widdershins**.

wifie a woman: *Get up and gie* (=give) *yir* (=your) *seat to that wifie.*

wilkies, tummle yir wilkies to turn a somersault, to go head over heels: *I slipped on the ice and nearly tummled ma wilkies*. [Other earlier forms of this include **tummle ower yir wullcats** and **tummle the wullcat**, a wullcat being a wild cat, and the phrases being a reference to this creature's agility]

willie-waught *(the gh is pronounced as the ch in loch)* a hearty swig of a drink, particularly an alcoholic one.

winch **1.** to go out with a member of the opposite sex on a regular basis, to be romantically involved with someone: *We don't see much of Jim in the pub; he's winchin'.* **2.** to kiss and cuddle: *They were winchin' in the back seat o' the car.* [The practice is now unisex, but the word comes from **wench**, a girl]

windae window: *a hoose* (=house) *wi* (=with) *big windaes.*

winna, winnae won't: *She winna care.*

wis was: *He wis filthy.*

wise *(pronounced to rhyme with nice)*, **no wise** not sensible: *He's no wise; he lent Dave money.*

wisna, wisnae wasn't: *She wisna sure*.

wrang wrong: *He did wrang* and *That's the wrang place*.

wulk a whelk or periwinkle. **fou as a wulk** very drunk. [*See* **fou**]

wumman, wummin a woman: *an old wumman at the bus stop*.

wur, wir 1. were: *We wir there*. 2. our: *Wir dug* (=dog) *got killed*.

wurna, wurnae weren't: *They wurnae there*.

wynd *(now found mainly in place names)* a narrow street or lane, often a winding one, leading off a major street: *Castle Wynd*.

Y

yammer to talk on and on, often loudly and often without saying anything important: *They were yammerin' away in the seat next to me and I was trying to read my book*.

yatter to talk incessantly, to chatter, often without saying anything of much importance: *They yattered away the whole journey*. [In origin the word imitates the sound made by people chattering away]

ye you: *Ye cannae* (=can't) *mean it*.

yett a gate.

yin one: *Ah'll* (=I'll) *have that yin*.

yokin' time the time at which work starts. *See* **lowsin' time**. [A reference to horses being yoked together at the start of ploughing]

yon that, those: *Yon lad's guilty*.

yon time very late: *It'll be yon time before we get finished at this rate.*

youse *(pronounced as **use**)* you (plural): *Will youse shut up!*

yowe a female sheep, a ewe: Burns' song *Ca the Yowes tae the Knowes.*